SUPERSTARS OF BASEBALL

ROBINSON CANÓ

THE RISE TO THE TOP!

Robinson Canó is a baseball superstar!

2012

Wins the Home Run Derby with his father.

2011

Wins the Silver Slugger Award and the Gold Glove Award.

2010

Signs a contract with the Yankees for 6 years and $55 million.

2008

Starts playing in the Major Leagues.

2005

The Yankees sign Canó to play in the minor leagues.

2001

Born in San Pedro de Macorís.

1982

Mason Crest
370 Reed Road
Broomall, Pennsylvania 19008
www.masoncrest.com

Printed and bound in the United States of America.

First printing
9 8 7 6 5 4 3 2 1

Library of Congress Cataloging-in-Publication Data

Rodríguez Gonzalez, Tania.
  Robinson Canó / by Tania Rodriguez.
     p. cm.
  Includes index.
  ISBN 978-1-4222-2683-4 (hardcover) -- ISBN 978-1-4222-2670-4 (series hardcover) -- ISBN 978-1-4222-9172-6 (ebook)
  1. Canó, Robinson, 1982---Juvenile literature. 2. Hispanic American baseball players--Biography--Juvenile literature. 3. Baseball players--United States--Biography--Juvenile literature. I. Title.
  GV865.C312R64 2012
  796.357092--dc23
  [B]
                                          2012021371

Produced by Harding House Publishing Services, Inc.
www.hardinghousepages.com

Picture Credits:
Adam Jones: p. 6
Keith Allison: p. 2, 27
Mangin, Brad: p. 1, 14, 15, 18, 20, 22, 24, 26, 28
Roman Snytsar | Dreamstime.com: p. 4
Ronald Callaghan | Dreamstime.com: p. 12

ROBINSON CANÓ

Chapter 1

Baseball, the Dominican Republic, and Robinson Canó

Robinson Canó hasn't been in baseball for very long, but he's already had a great career. Canó has done many things some players will never get the chance to do. He's won the World Series and played in an *All-Star Game*. He's won awards and made millions of dollars. Few players get to do the things that Canó has done in just a few years in *Major League Baseball (MLB)*.

Like this boy, Robinson loved base- ball from a young age.

Today, fans know Canó for his hard work. They know him for his success at batting and his strong play on **defense**. Fans know Canó for his Home Run Derby win in 2011.

Canó wasn't always the player that fans know today, though. He's had to work hard to make it to where he is now. Canó's path to playing in the Major Leagues started many years ago in the Dominican Republic. The island's rich baseball culture helped to make him the superstar he is today.

The History of Dominican Baseball

Historians aren't exactly sure how baseball first came to the island, but they know it's been there since at least 1880.

Americans brought the game of baseball to the Caribbean in the mid-1860s when U.S. business interests grew in Cuba, one of the Dominican Republic's neighbors. Then, between 1868 and 1878, many Cubans fled their country during the Ten Years' War. Many of them ended up in the Dominican Republic. They brought the game of baseball with them—and it caught on fast!

Today, every baseball fan knows the fairy tale about the Dominican boy who grew up barefoot, using a milk carton for a baseball glove, a broom handle for a bat, and rolled up socks or lemons for balls—and somehow was transformed into a "Big Papi," a Vlad Guerrero, or a Robinson Canó. But the fairy godmoth-

Steroids

For many professional players, the pressure to perform well is intense. Athletes face stress from everyone around them to constantly improve their skill, strength, and speed in the game of baseball. From the fans who want their favorite players to win and score good stats, to the coaches and team managers who push their players to perform to their maximum potential, to the players themselves, who are surrounded by other world-class athletes and feel the need to overcome them, the pressure to excel is extreme. Often, an athlete turns to chemical enhancements to reach a level of competitive play that he would not normally be capable of. This is never legal, and is almost always dangerous, but nevertheless, many Major League players feel compelled to participate in performance-enhancing drug use.

The most common performance enhancers are anabolic steroids. These chemicals are similar to testosterone, which is the male hormone naturally produced by the body to help stimulate muscle growth. That's why when a player takes anabolic steroids, he receives a boost to his speed and strength that is greater than what the body could normally produce on its own. Major League Baseball (MLB), as well as almost every other organized sport, considers this cheating.

Steroids can cause an unhealthy increase in cholesterol levels and an increase in blood pressure. This stresses the heart, and leads to an increased risk of heart disease. Large doses of steroids can also lead to liver failure, and they have a negative effect on blood sugar levels, sometimes causing problems similar to diabetes.

If an adolescent (typically someone under the age of about 17) takes anabolic steroids, the risks are often much worse. Steroids stop bones from growing, which results in stunted growth. In addition, the risks to the liver and heart are much greater, since a young person's liver and heart are not fully matured and are more susceptible to the damage that steroids can cause. Furthermore, taking steroids puts you at a greater risk of psychological problems that generally begin with aggression but often lead to much more serious issues. Considering these health risks, as well as the fact that anabolic steroids are almost universally banned from organized sports, they should not be used, except by those who have legitimate medical conditions that require their use.

er in this tale—the one who makes this magical transformation take place—is the "buscón"—the Dominican coach or trainer—and he's sometimes as much a villain as a savior!

Buscones often lie about their players' ages. (Legally, a Major League Baseball team can't sign a boy until he's at least 16.) They sometimes keep the boys out of school and inject them with steroids to make them grow bigger. The buscones may take most of the boys' signing bonuses, without the boys even knowing. Sometimes, they bribe the scouts. Several scouts and officials from the Yankees, Red Sox, and Nationals have even lost their jobs because of their dealings with buscones.

The American baseball leagues first became interested in the Dominican Republic back in the 1960s. At first, teams would sign players for $2,000, with a $500 tip to the buscón, but that changed in the 1990s when pitcher Ricardo Aramboles was signed for $1 million. Suddenly, top prospects were now worth six or even seven figures— and buscones could make real money,

Jesús, Matty, and Felipe Alou in 1963.

opening the door to greedy individuals ready to take advantage of the system.

The leagues sent money, players, and scouts to the island. Dominican baseball players had the chance now to sharpen their skills against some of the world's best talent. Baseball schools opened across the island, offering boys the chance to learn to play ball. Some of these schools were good, some were bad. The best ones gave boys like Robinson Canó the chance to make it big. Today, every team in Major League Baseball has a school or some other presence in the Dominican Republic. Baseball ties the United States and the Dominican Republic together.

And as people around the world pay more and more attention to Dominican baseball, more buscones are operating like legitimate agents and trainers. And despite the corruption, the fairy tales do come true for some lucky boys, boys like Robinson Canó, who make it big in the world of baseball.

By 2011, 420 players from the Dominican Republic had played in the Major Leagues. More Dominicans play in the Majors than players from any other country in Latin America. In fact, the Dominican Republic has more players in the Majors than all other coun-

tries in Latin America combined. Dominicans are leaving their mark on other aspects of the game as well. In 2003, Tony Peña, who once played for the Kansas City Royals, coached against Felipe Alou, of the San Francisco Giants, making it the first time that two Dominicans coached against each other in the Major Leagues. And then, in 2004, Omar Minaya became the first Dominican General Manager, working the front office for the New York Mets. Dominicans are first-class leaders in the world of baseball!

Today, the strength of Dominican baseball is found in each of the Major League's 30 teams. And at the same time, baseball is still just as popular in this Latin American county. Robinson Canó and all the other Dominican players in the Majors inspire the little boys who play ball in the streets of the Dominican Republic. These boys dream about being the next A-Rod—or Robinson Canó.

Players like Robinson Canó prove that dreams can come true!

Robinson's Early Life

Robinson Canó was born on October 22, 1982. He was born in San Pedro de Macorís in the Dominican Republic.

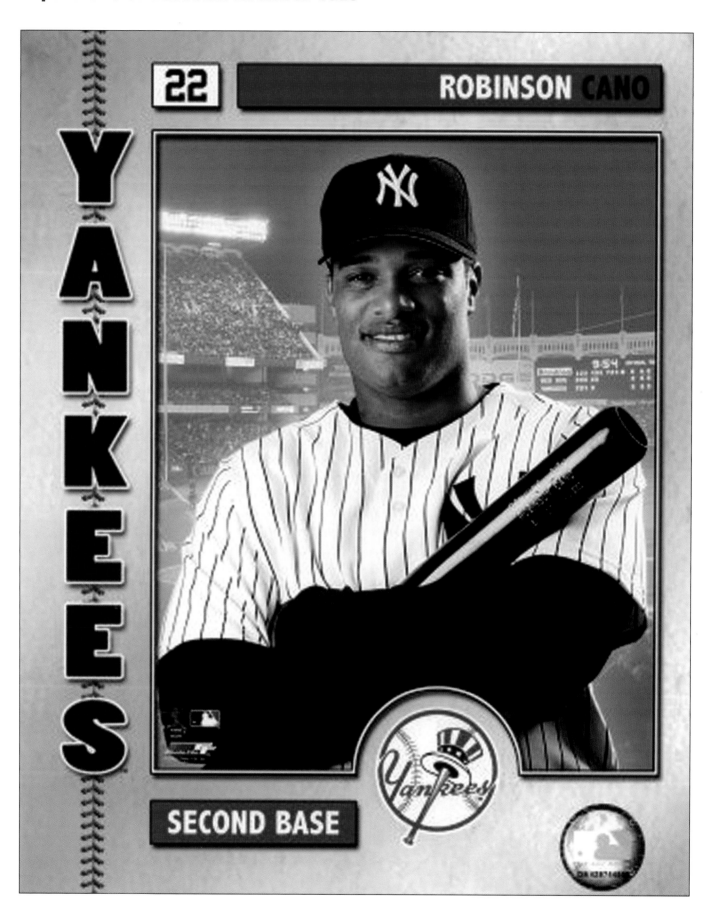

It All Started in a Sugarcane Field. . .

"I'm not sure why I started it," says Epy Guerrero, who founded his country's first baseball academy, in Villa Mella in 1973. "Perhaps it was an inspiration from God. I thought to myself, If these kids had some guidance, maybe they could succeed."

A former minor leaguer, Guerrero came up with the idea while scouting for the Astros. The academy started out as just a small field and a house for himself and his players in a patch of cleared jungle—but by 1978, the Toronto Blue Jays were using his expanding facility. Guerrero signed more than 60 players who reached the Major Leagues, and other teams started to pay attention, especially the Dodgers. Today, 29 Major League teams have Dominican academies, but the Dodgers' facility, built on what had once been a sugarcane field, was the first of its kind.

Robinson's father's name was José Canó. His mother's name was Claribel. José was a baseball player. He loved baseball. He even named his son after his favorite baseball player, Jackie Robinson.

When Robinson was young, he didn't see much of his father. José was trying to become a Major League pitcher. He was working hard to follow his dream of playing baseball for a living.

In 1987, the Houston Astros **signed** José to a **minor league contract**. He spent the next few years playing in the United States. He even got to play for in the big leagues for a few games in 1989. José never quite made it into the Majors. But he did get to keep playing baseball in leagues around the world until 1999.

When Robinson was 13 years old, he and his family moved to the United States. Robinson lived in Newark, New Jersey. He went to school there for 3 years.

Robinson and his family soon moved back to the Dominican Republic. There, Robinson went to San Pedro Apostol High School. The school was in San Pedro de Macorís. Robinson loved sports and played baseball and basketball in high school.

Robinson was very good at baseball. He'd learned a lot from his father. And he'd worked hard to be as good a player as he could be. Soon, **scouts** were looking at Robinson. A scout from the Yankees, Carlos Rios, watched Robinson closely. He knew Robinson could be a great player. Robinson knew it too.

11

Chapter 2

BREAKING INTO BASEBALL

In 2001, the Yankees signed Robinson to a minor league contract. Robinson would have to work through the Yankees' farm teams. Soon, he'd have his chance to play in the Major Leagues. But first, he'd have to spend some time playing in the minors.

Starting in the Minors

In 2001, Canó played for the Gulf Coast League (GCL) Yankees. The team plays in the Rookie League. Canó played in 57 games for the GCL Yankees. In that time, he scored 37 runs and had 34 *runs batted in (RBIs)*. He hit 3 home runs for the team. Canó's *batting average* was .230.

At the end of the 2001 season, the Yankees moved Canó to another team, the Staten Island Yankees. Canó played just two games with his new team that year.

Canó started the 2002 season with the Staten Island Yankees. He played 22 games for the team that year. After that, the Yankees moved Canó again. This time, he was playing with the Greensboro Bats from North Carolina. Canó played in 113 games for the Bats in 2002. He scored 67 runs and had 66 RBIs. He hit 14 home runs. Canó's batting average was .321.

In 2003, Canó played for two teams again. He started with the Tampa Yankees. He played 90 games for the Florida team. He scored 50 runs and had 50 RBIs. Then, Canó moved to the Trenton (New Jersey) Thunder. He played in 46 games for the Thunder.

In 2004, Canó began the season with the Thunder. He played in 74 games for the team in 2004. He scored 43 runs and had 44 RBIs. His batting average was .301. Soon, the Yankees moved Canó to the Columbus Clippers. The Clippers are a Class AAA team. Canó played in 61 games for the team. He scored 22 runs and had 30 RBIs. His batting average was .259.

The Yankees almost *traded* Canó in 2004. But the team ended up keeping him after deals with other teams changed. The Yankees didn't know it then, but the team was lucky to keep Canó!

Going to the Big Leagues

In 2005, Canó finally got his chance to play in the Major Leagues. He started the season on the Columbus Clippers again. He played 24 games with Columbus. During that time, he scored 19 runs and had 24 RBIs. He hit four home runs. Canó's batting average was .333.

In May, the Yankees brought Canó up from the minors. Finally, Canó had made it to the Major Leagues. He'd reached his dream of playing in the Majors.

In the 2005 regular season, Canó played in 132 games for the Yankees. He scored 78 runs and had 62 RBIs. He also hit 14 home runs. Canó's batting average was .297. At second base, Canó helped make 77 double plays. His fielding percentage was .974.

The Yankees had an amazing season in 2005. The team won 95 games and lost 67. The Yankees finished the season tied for first with their rivals, the Boston Red Sox. In the end, the Yankees won the **division** because the team had beaten Boston more times than they'd lost.

In 2005, the Yankees brought Canó up from the minors.

Robinson plays second base for the Yankees.

The Yankees went on to the American League Division Series (ALDS) to face the Los Angeles Angels. The Angels ended up beating the Yankees in the series. The Yankees' season was over.

Canó had finally broken into the Major Leagues. He'd even made it to the post-season in his rookie year! At the end of the season, Canó finished second in the voting for American League Rookie of the Year. He might not have won the award, but he did have a great first year in the big leagues.

Chapter 3

PLAYING FOR THE YANKEES

C anó's rookie year had been great. He'd played very well. He'd almost been the Rookie of the Year. Canó was ready to work hard to keep it up.

_____

Canó in New York

Canó started the 2006 season strong. But in July he hurt his leg. Canó missed playing most of the month. He also missed that year's All-Star Game, even though he was a favorite to play second base for the American League.

Canó came back in August. And he played very well. He won American League Player of the Month in September. He helped the Yankees finish the season first in the team's division. The team won 97 games and lost 65. The Yankees faced the Detroit Tigers in the American League Division Series. The Tigers won the series three games to one.

In the 2006 regular season, Canó played in 122 games for the Yankees. He scored 62 runs and had 78 RBIs. He hit 15 home runs. Canó's batting average was .342. Canó had missed a month because of his hurt leg. But he still put up great numbers. Only two players had better batting averages than Canó in 2006.

Canó started at second base in 115 games. His fielding percentage was .984. Canó helped make 73 double plays in 2006.

In the 2007 season, Canó changed the number on his uniform. He gave the number 22 to Roger Clemens. Canó asked the Yankees if he could wear the number 24. Jackie Robinson wore number 42. He had been Canó's father's favorite player. And Canó had been named after Jackie Robinson.

Canó had an amazing season in 2007. He played in 160 games for the Yankees in 2007. He scored 93 runs and had 97 RBIs. Canó hit 19 home runs. His batting average was .306.

At second base, Canó started in 157 games. He helped make 136 double plays in 2007. His fielding percentage was .984.

The Yankees had a strong season. But they didn't win their division. The Yankees won 94 games and lost 68 in 2007. The Boston Red Sox won two more games than the Yankees. The Red Sox won the division.

The Yankees did win the Wild Card, though. The Yankees played the Cleveland Indians in the ALDS. The Indians ended up winning the series. The Yankees won just one game. The team would have to try again in the next season.

Staying with the Yankees

Early in 2008, Canó signed another contract with the Yankees. He agreed to play for the team for 6 seasons. The Yankees agreed to pay Canó $55 million over 6

19

Robinson Canó is someone who plays with everything he has.

seasons. Canó was staying with the team that brought him into the Majors.

In the 2008 season, Canó played in 159 games for the Yankees. He scored 70 runs and had 72 RBIs. He hit 14 home runs. Canó's batting average was .271.

Canó started at third base in 154 games in 2008. He helped make 103 double plays during the season. His fielding percentage was .984. He'd had the same percentage in 2007.

The Yankees didn't have the best year in 2008. They won 89 games and lost 73.

The team finished third in the American League East Division. The Yankees didn't make it to the playoffs in 2008. This was the first year that they hadn't made it to the playoffs since 1992!

Canó hadn't had his best season either. His numbers were lower than in 2007. Some fans wondered whether he'd tried his best. Canó didn't like hearing that at all. He knew he'd have to work harder in the next season.

Chapter 4

CANÓ AT THE TOP

C anó wasn't happy with the way he'd played in 2008. In 2009, he was ready to show fans that he could do better. The Yankees were ready to do better too.

A Big Year

Canó played much better in 2009 than he had in 2008. In the 2009 regular season, Canó scored 103 runs. He had 85 RBIs and hit 25 home runs. Canó's batting average was .320 in 2009. He started at second base in 161 games. His fielding percentage was .984 for the third year in a row.

The Yankees had a much better year too. The team finished at the top of the American League East. The Yankees won an amazing 103 games. The team lost just 59. The Yankees hadn't made it to the playoffs in 2008. But now, the team was headed to the post-season.

In the American League Division Series, the Yankees played the Minnesota Twins. The Yankees won 3 games in a row to end the series. The Yankees played the Los Angeles Angels in the American League Championship Series (ALCS). In the sixth game of the series, the Yankees beat the Angels. The Yankees won the ALCS and were headed to the World Series.

The Yankees played the Philadelphia Phillies in the 2009 *World Series*. The series lasted for 6 games. In the end, the Yankees beat the Phillies in Game 6 to win the Series.

Canó had reached the top of baseball. He'd won a World Series. Many players dream their whole lives of winning the World Series. Canó had done it after just a few years in the Majors.

Staying Successful

Canó had a strong start to the 2010 season. He won the American League Player of the Month award in April. He was chosen to play in the All-Star Game later in the year, too. Canó couldn't join in the Home Run Derby in 2010, though. He was hurt and couldn't play. The injury didn't stop him from finishing a great season with the Yankees, though.

The Yankees finished second in the American League East in 2010. The team won 95 games and lost 67. But the Yankees won the Wild Card and made it to the playoffs anyway.

At the end of the regular season, Canó scored 103 runs. He had 109 RBIs and hit 29 home runs in 2010. His batting average was .319. At second base, Canó's fielding percentage was .996. He helped make 114 double plays.

The Yankees played the Minnesota Twins in the ALDS. The Yankees won the series in 3 games. In the American League Championship Series, the

It's important to Canó that he can consider himself a good person.

Yankees played the Texas Rangers. The Rangers ended up winning the series after 6 games. The Yankees had won the World Series in 2009. And the team came close to making it into the World Series again in 2010. But the team's season was over after the ALCS.

At the end of the 2010 season, Canó won the Silver Slugger Award. He also won the Gold Glove Award. Canó came in third for voting on the American League's Most Valuable Player.

In 2011, Canó played 159 games with the Yankees. He scored 104 runs and had 118 RBIs. Canó hit 28 home runs. His batting average was .302. On **defense**, Canó helped make 97 double plays at second base. His fielding percentage was .987.

Canó was chosen to play in the 2011 All-Star Game. He started on second base in the game. Canó was also given the chance to be in the Home Run Derby in 2011. Canó chose his father to pitch to him in the Home Run Derby.

Canó ended up winning the Derby. He couldn't be happier.

"I don't want to say that I won this trophy," Canó said after he won. "I want to say that my dad has won this trophy."

Canó and his father had practiced together for years. But this time, they had worked together to win the Home Run Derby in front of millions of fans.

"This is a good memory," Canó said after the Derby. "It's something that I'm always going to have in my mind and my heart."

The Yankees played well in the 2011 season. The team finished first in the American League East division. The Yankees won 97 games and lost 65 in 2011. The team went to the playoffs to face the Detroit Tigers. The Yankees lost the ALDS to the Tigers in Game 5.

The Yankees didn't make it to the World Series in 2011. But Canó had one of his best seasons yet. He'd played in the All-Star Game and won the Home Run Derby. Canó was playing great and making Yankees fans happy.

Chapter 5

ROBINSON CANÓ TODAY

R obinson Canó has reached many heights in baseball other players can only dream about. He's won a World Series. He's played in All-Star Games a few times. He's won awards and made millions of dollars. Canó even won the 2011 Home Run Derby! Few players can say they've done as much as Canó.

Baseball is very important to Cano. But it's not the only thing that matters to him. Cano has been able to find success in baseball and also keep in mind what's most important to him.

Cano's family is very important to him. At the 2011 Home Run Derby, Cano even brought his father, José, along to pitch to him! Cano learned his love of baseball from his father. And he's never forgotten who he got his passion from. Cano is close with his mother and father. He's stayed close to his Dominican roots, even while in the United States.

Cano knows that success isn't much if you don't use it to help others. Giving back is very important to him. He's worked with the Yankees to give to charity for years. He's also worked to help

Canó won a lot of awards in 2010.

children in need in the Dominican Republic. Cano held a fundraiser for Dominican children with heart disease.

When Cano won the Home Run Derby in 2011, he talked about what's most important to him:

"It don't matter how much money you make or how long you play," Cano said. "Those are the kind of things, the memories that you can bring home and always share with your family—not only now, but when you retire. You can look over and say, 'Wow, I was good back in the day.'"

No one can say for sure what's next for Robinson Cano. But he will keep working hard to play his best. Cano will also keep in mind what's important to him. He'll keep his family close. He'll keep giving back to those in need. No matter what happens next, Cano will stay true to himself.

Find Out More

Online

Baseball Almanac
www.baseball-almanac.com

Baseball Hall of Fame
baseballhall.org

Baseball Reference
www.baseball-reference.com

Dominican Baseball
mlb.mlb.com/mlb/features/dr/
index.jsp

History of Baseball
www.19cbaseball.com

Major League Baseball
www.mlb.com

Science of Baseball
www.exploratorium.edu/baseball

In Books

Augustin, Bryan. *The Dominican Republic From A to Z.* New York: Scholastic, 2005.

Jacobs, Greg. *The Everything Kids' Baseball Book.* Avon, Mass.: F+W Media, 2012.

Kurlansky, Mark. *The Eastern Stars: How Baseball Changed the Dominican Town of San Pedro de Macorís.* New York: Riverhead Books, 2010.

Glossary

All-Star Game: The game played in July between the best players from each of the two leagues within the MLB.

batting average: A statistic that measures how good a batter is, which is calculated by dividing the number of hits a player gets by how many times he is at bat.

contract: A written promise between a player and the team. It tells how much he will be paid for how long.

culture: The way of life of a group of people, which includes things like values and beliefs, language, food, and art.

defense: Playing to keep the other team from scoring; includes the outfield and infield positions, pitcher, and catcher.

disabled list: A list of players who are injured and can't play for a certain period of time.

division: A group of teams that plays one another to compete for the championship; in the MLB, divisions are based on geographic regions.

free agent: A player who does not currently have a contract with any team.

general manager: The person in charge of a baseball team, who is responsible for guiding the team to do well.

heritage: Something passed down by previous generations.

Major League Baseball (MLB): The highest level of professional baseball in the United States and Canada.

minor leagues: The level of professional baseball right below the Major Leagues.

Most Valuable Player (MVP): The athlete who is named the best player for a certain period of time.

offense: Playing to score runs at bat.

playoffs: A series of games played after the regular season ends, to determine who will win the championship.

professional: The level of baseball in which players get paid.

rookie: A player in his first-year in the MLB.

runs batted in (RBI): The number of points that a player gets for his team by hitting the ball.

scouts: People who find the best young baseball players to sign to teams.

sign: To agree to a contract between a baseball player and a team.

trade: An agreement with another team that gives a player in return for a player from the other team.

Index